Letter Formation Chart

 Aa Bb Cc Dd

Ee Ff Gg Hh

Ii Jj Kk Ll

Mm Nn Oo Pp

Qq Rr Ss Tt

Uu Vv Ww Xx

Yy Zz

anteater

A A A
A a A a
a a
A A A
a a a

bat

B B B
b b b
A B a b
B b B b
A B a b

EMC 6844 • © Evan-Moor Corp.

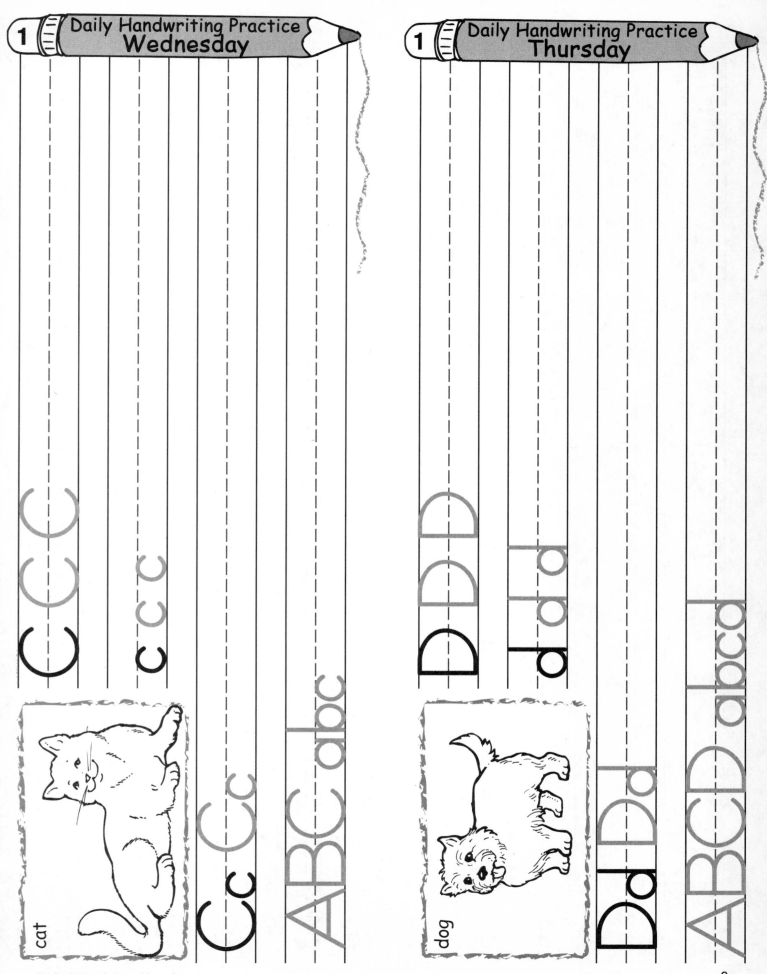

C C C

c c c

Cc Cc

ABC abc

cat

D D D

d d d

Dd Dd

ABCD abcd

dog

Copy the letters.

Aa   Bb   Cc   Dd

Aa

Bb

Cc

Dd

Dad   bad

dab   cab

4

E E E

e e e

E e

a b c d e

E e E

elephant

F F F

f f f

F f D d

C c B b A a

fox

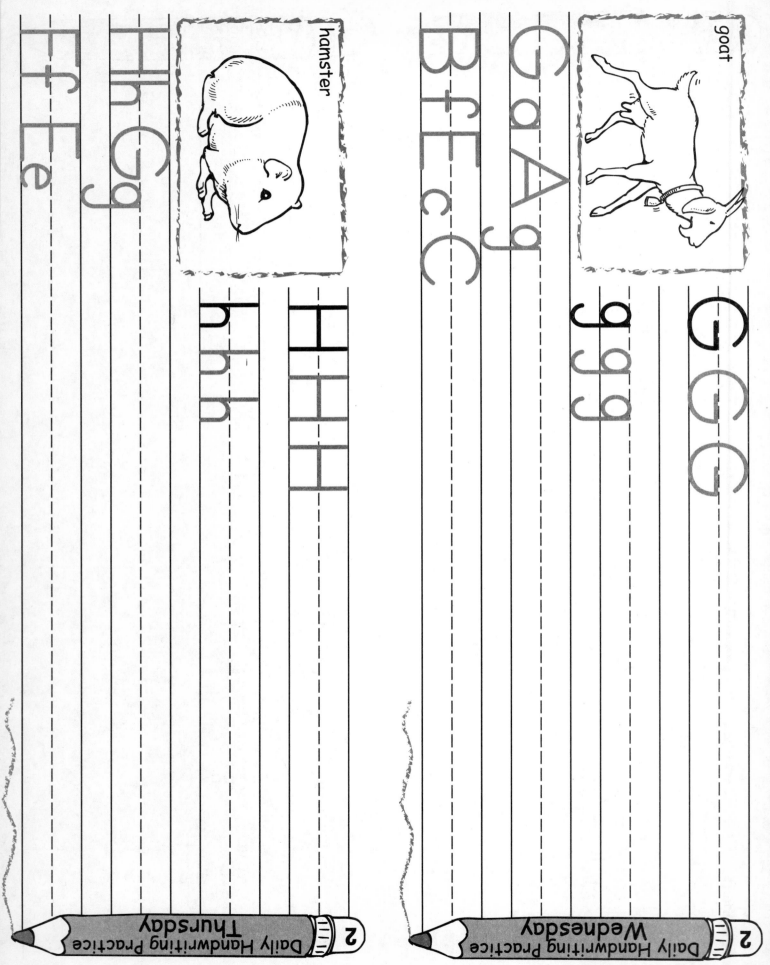

goat

G G G
ggg

GaAg
BfEcC

hamster

Hh Gg
FfEe

HHH
hhh

EMC 6844 • © Evan-Moor Corp.

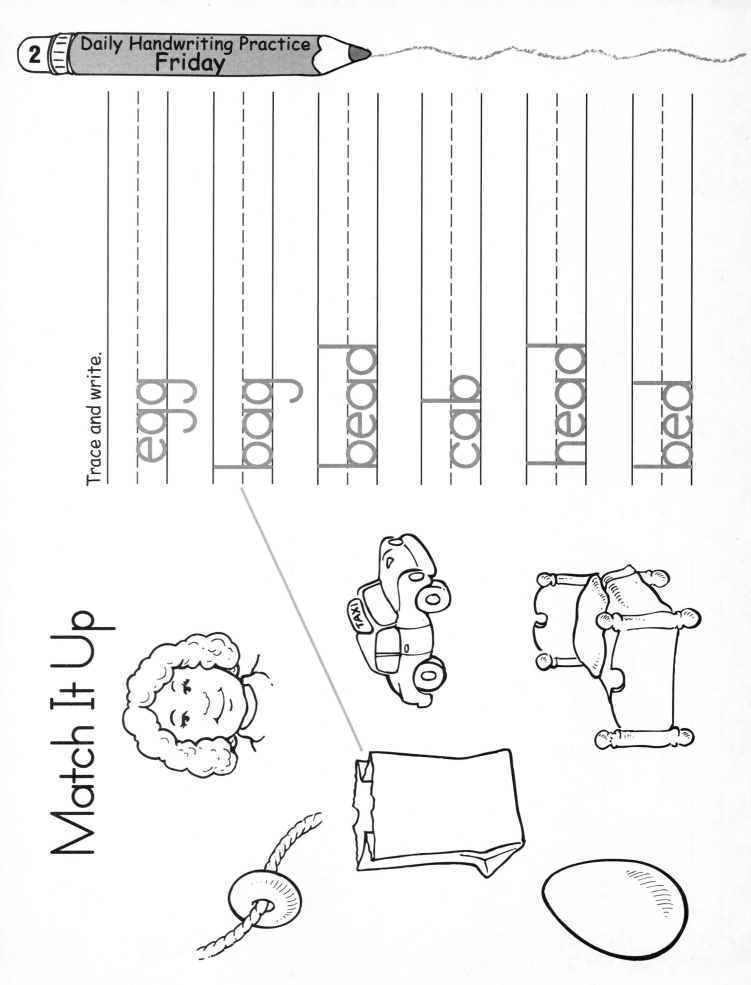

Trace and write.

egg

bag

bead

cab

head

bed

Match It Up

I i

hide
hide
hide.

J j

jab
jab.
jab.

8

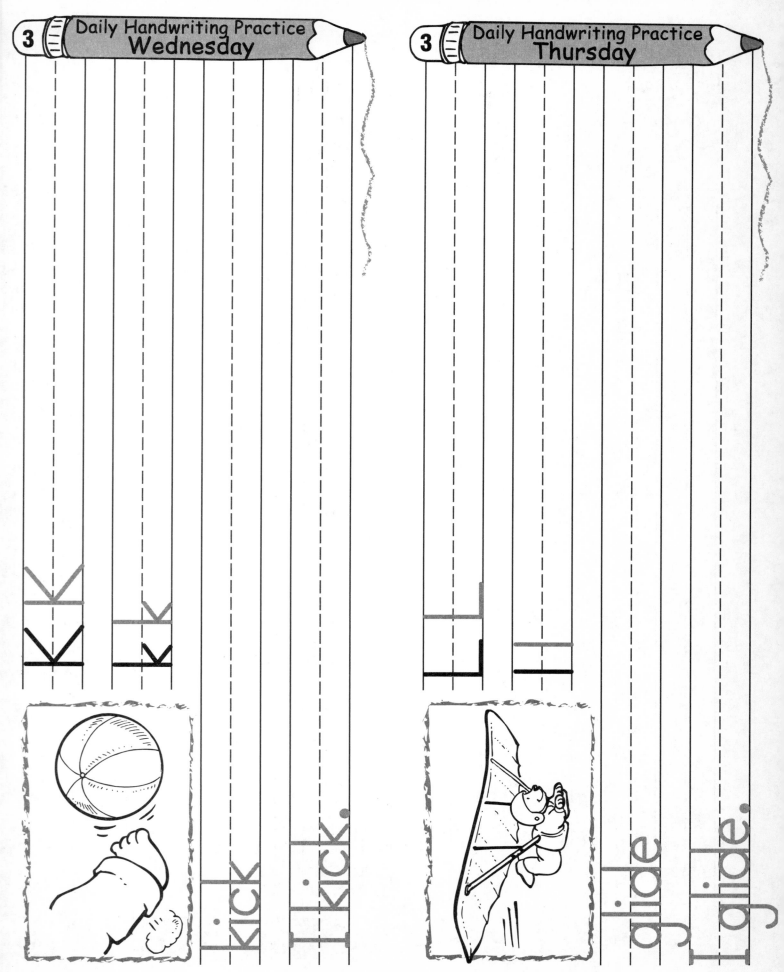

K K
K K

kick
I kick.

L l
L l

glide
I glide.

Things I Can Do

Trace and write.

I hide.

I kick.

I glide.

I jab.

I lace.

I dig.

I beg.

MM

m m

MMMmmm!

I like cake.

Mmmm!

NN

n n

Nice!

Neckties are nice.

Nice!

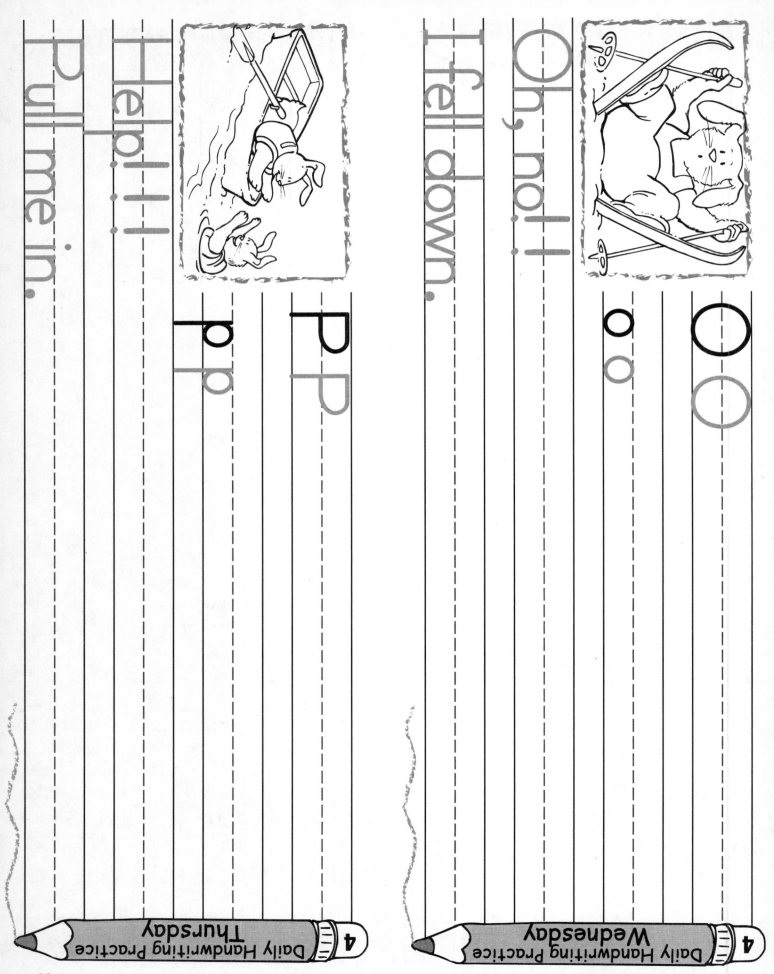

Oh, no!!

I fell down.

O O

o o

Help!!!

Pull me in.

P P

p p

12

Ben Digs

Can Ben find a map?
Can Ben find a bone?

Can Ben find a map?

Dig, Ben, Dig.
Dig deep.
Find a bone.

Good job, Ben.

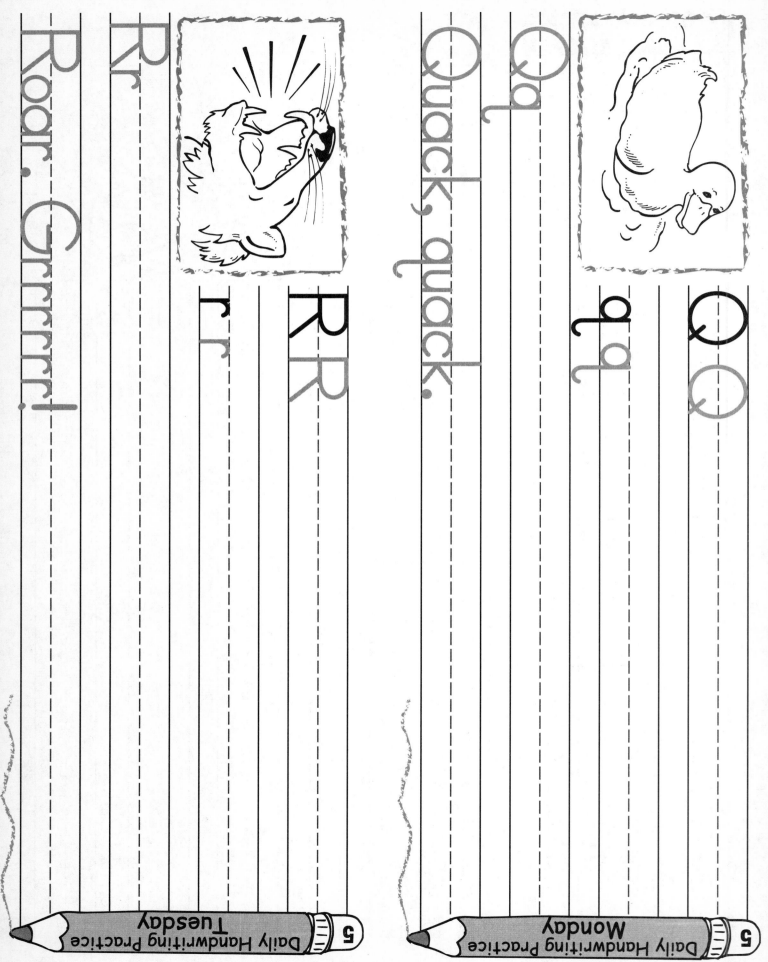

Monday

Qq

Qq

Qq

qq

Quack, quack.

Tuesday

Rr

Rr

RR

r r

Roar, Grrrrr!

Ss Ss

s s

Eeeee!

Ss

Scream.

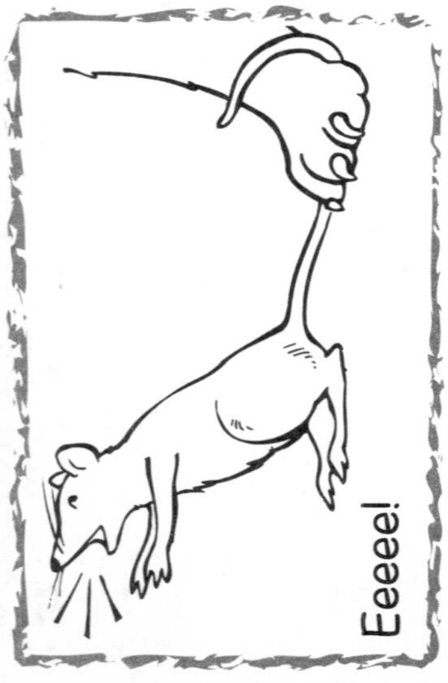

Tt Tt

t t

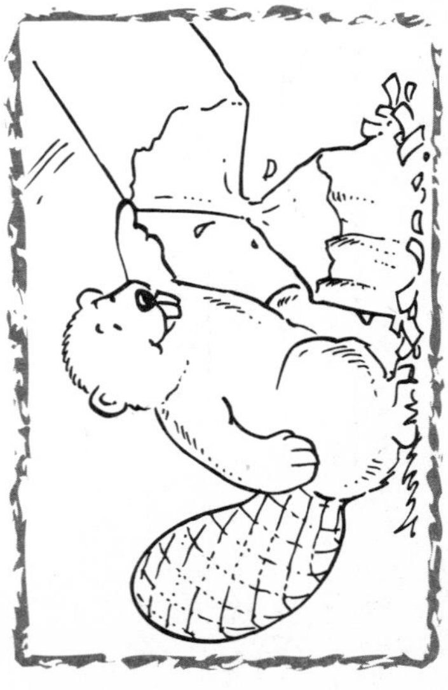

Tt

Timber!

Trace

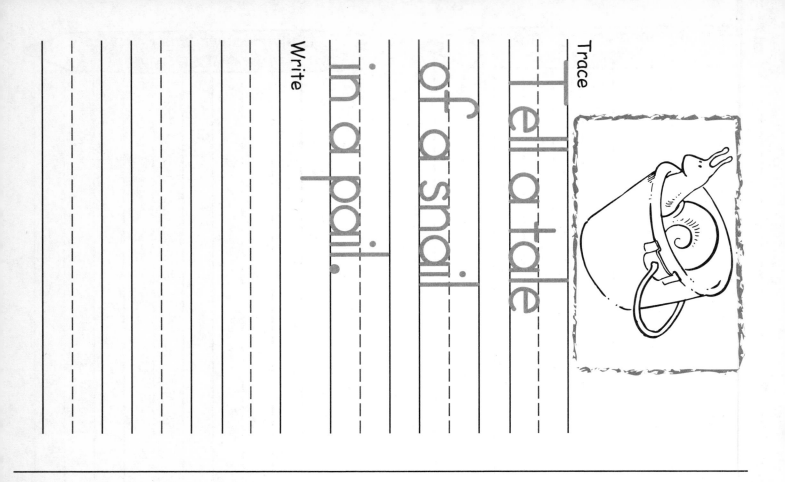

Tell a tale
of a snail
in a pail.

Write

_____

Make a wish
for a fish
on a dish.

Write

_____

U u
u u

under

The kitten is under the table.

V v
v v

over

Swing over the river, Fido.

X

X marks the spot on the map!

Xx

Xx

x x

W

Where is Willy the worm?

Where

Ww

w w

The glass holds two cups.
Excellent!

The glass holds two cups.

The pan holds one quart.
Excellent!

The tub holds two wet pups.
Do you have a towel?

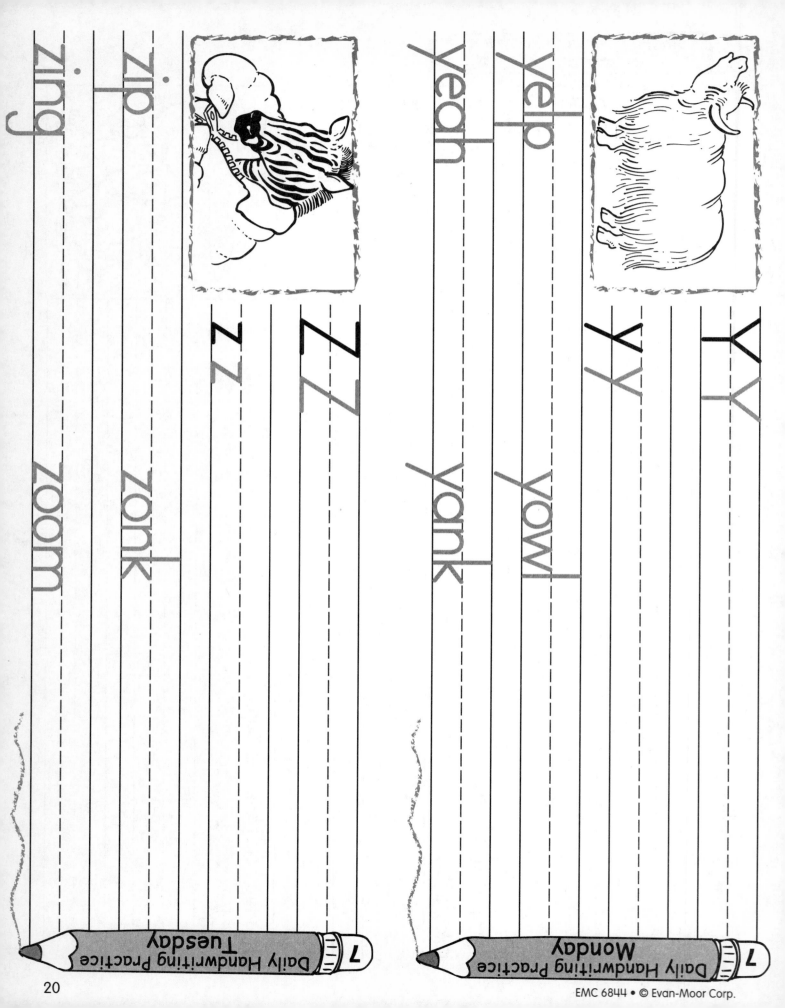

Zz

zing
zip
zoom
zonk

Yy

yeah
yep
yank
yow

one two three

I can count 1, 2, 3.

four five six

I can count 1, 2, 3, 4, 5, 6.

1 2 3

1 2 3   4 5 6

Trace and write.

Yes, please.

No, thank you.

Would you like some?

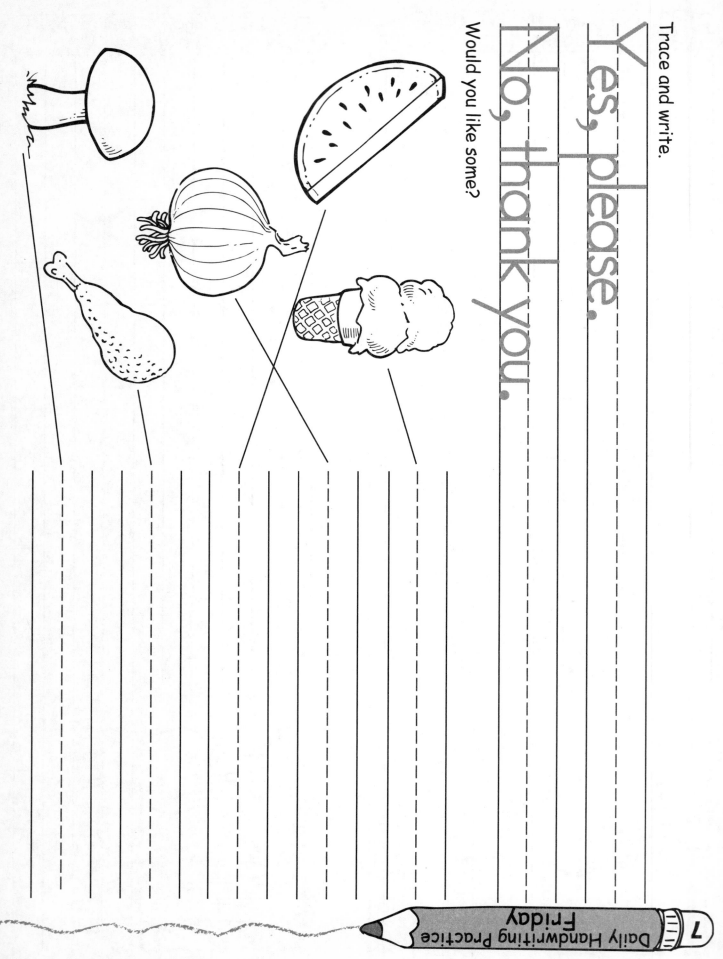

Daily Handwriting Practice
Friday

7

EMC 6844 • © Evan-Moor Corp.

b   u   e

blue

The blue morpho has two wings.

r   e   d

red

Roses are red, violets are blue.

The purple plums are sweet.

purple

p u r p l e

The yellow lemons are sour.

yellow

y e l l o w

EMC 6844 • © Evan-Moor Corp.

Color and write.

Mister Clown

red
yellow
blue
purple

The clown's hat is _____.

The clown's tie is _____.

The clown's nose is _____.

The clown's hair is _____.

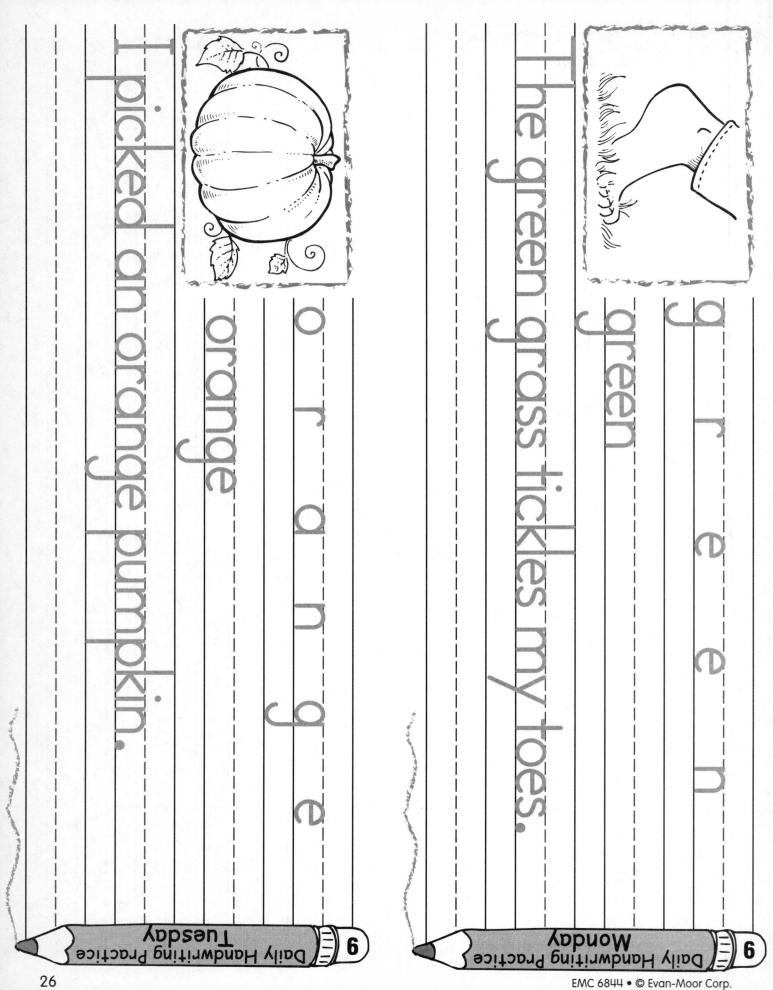

The green grass tickles my toes.

green

g r e e n

I picked an orange pumpkin.

orange

o r a n g e

p   i   n   k

pink

The pink piglets are cute.

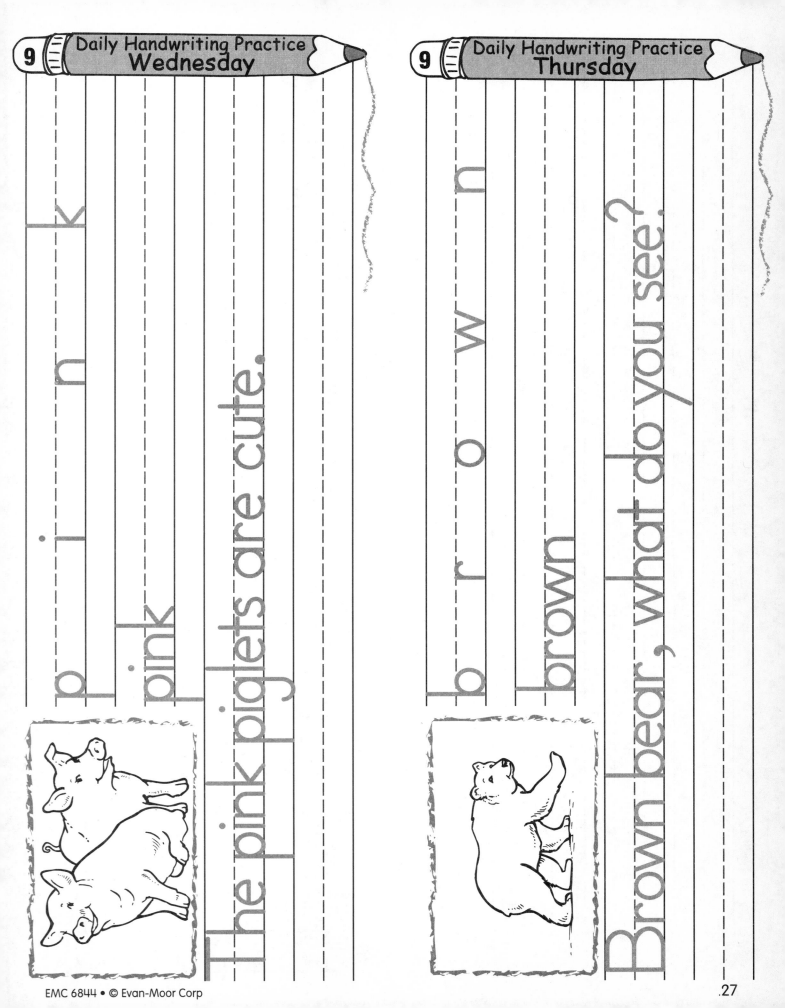

b   r   o   w   n

brown

Brown bear, what do you see?

The Color Wheel

Color and write.

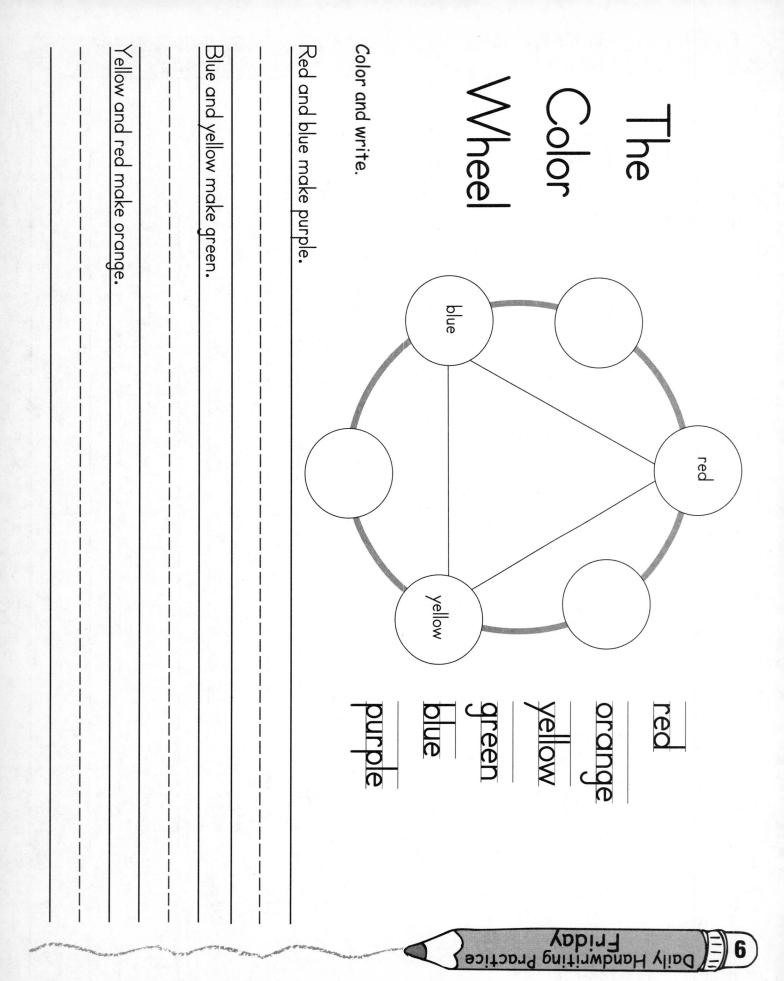

red
orange
yellow
green
blue
purple

Red and blue make purple.

- - - - - - - - - -

Blue and yellow make green.

- - - - - - - - - -

Yellow and red make orange.

- - - - - - - - - -

my book

your book

We like to share our books.

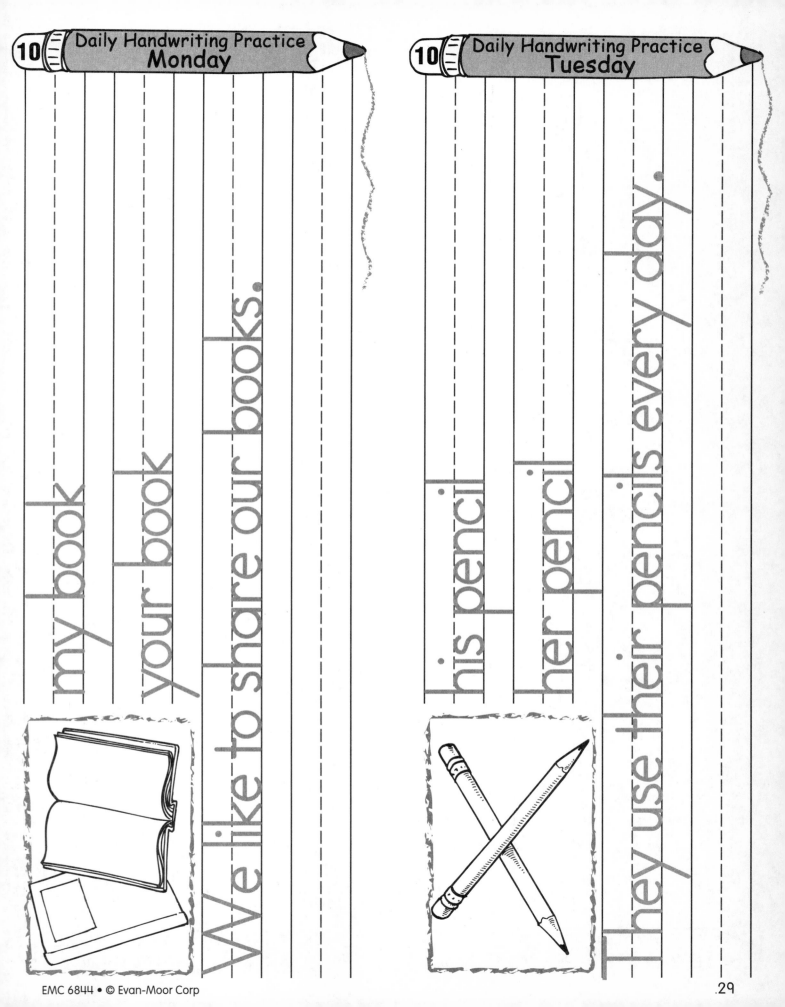

his pencil

her pencil

They use their pencils every day.

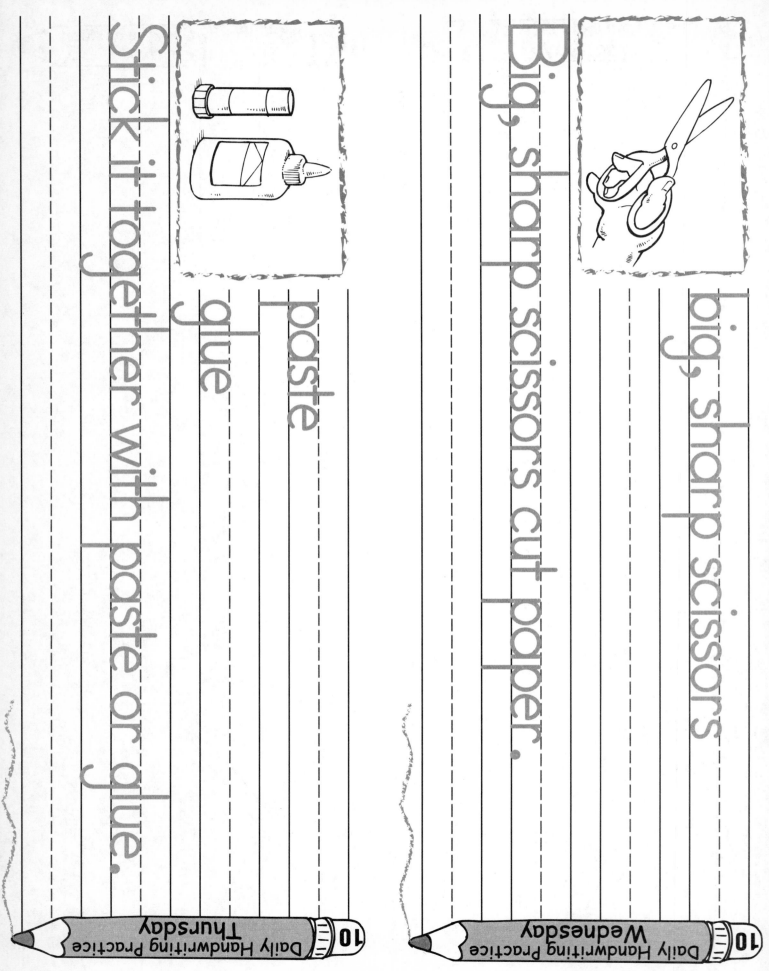

big, sharp scissors

Big, sharp scissors cut paper.

paste

glue

Stick it together with paste or glue.

At School

We use tools to help us at school.

We use scissors to cut.

We use pencils to write.

We use glue and paste to stick things together.

Copy the story.

Muff loves to run and jump.

rope

skip

Mac will catch the football.

score

kick

sit up

beg

Did Buster wag his tail?

Good for you.

sing

talk

Can you listen to the parrot?

Shhhh.

Copy the poem.

Frogs Hop

We go fast and we go slow.
Watch and see how fast we go.
Run and jump and skip and hop.
We go fast and never stop.

toast

cereal

I eat a balanced breakfast.

soup

sandwich

I eat a nutritious lunch.

C

dinner

supper

Come and get it. It's ready.

I

chips

fruit

I love to eat tasty snacks.

36

Lettuce Roll-up

Wash one lettuce leaf.
Spread peanut butter on it.
Sprinkle with raisins.
Roll up the leaf.
Eat and enjoy.

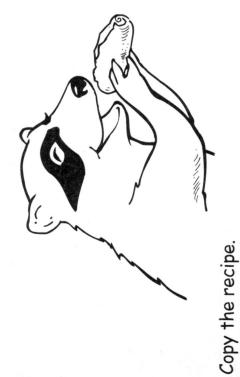

Copy the recipe.

These babies are called cubs.

lions

tigers

These animals like water.

hippo

elephant

zebra

giraffe

One has spots. One has stripes.

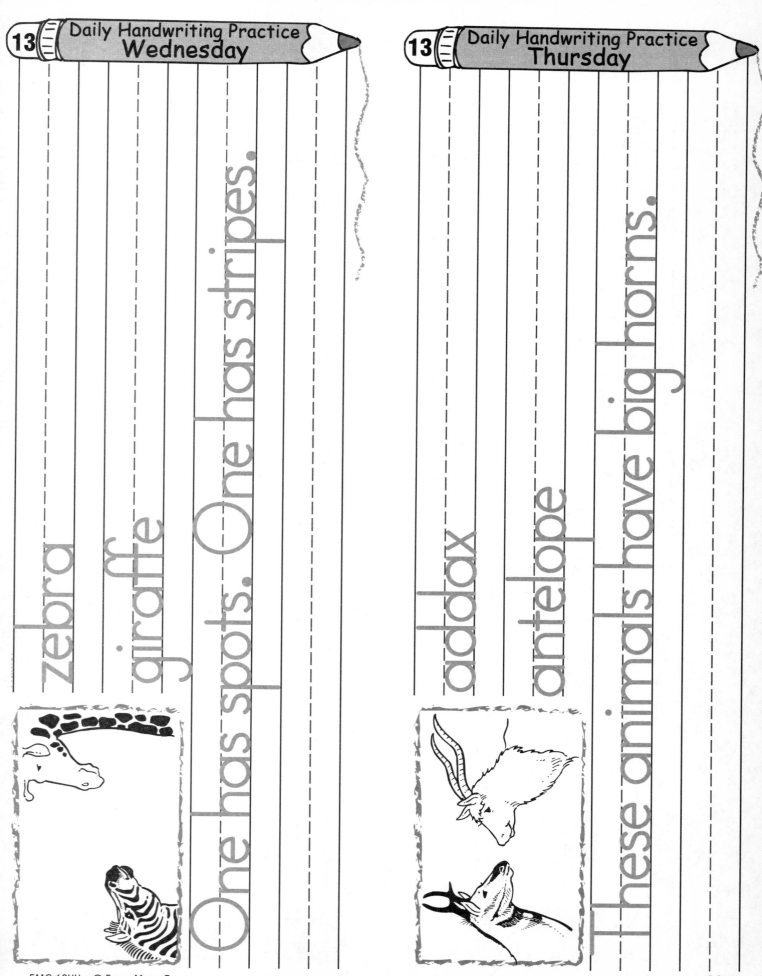

addax

antelope

These animals have big horns.

Welcome to the Zoo

hippo

elephant

lion

tiger

addax

antelope

giraffe

zebra

Once upon a time

a beautiful princess lived...

in a lonely castle

surrounded by a deep moat.

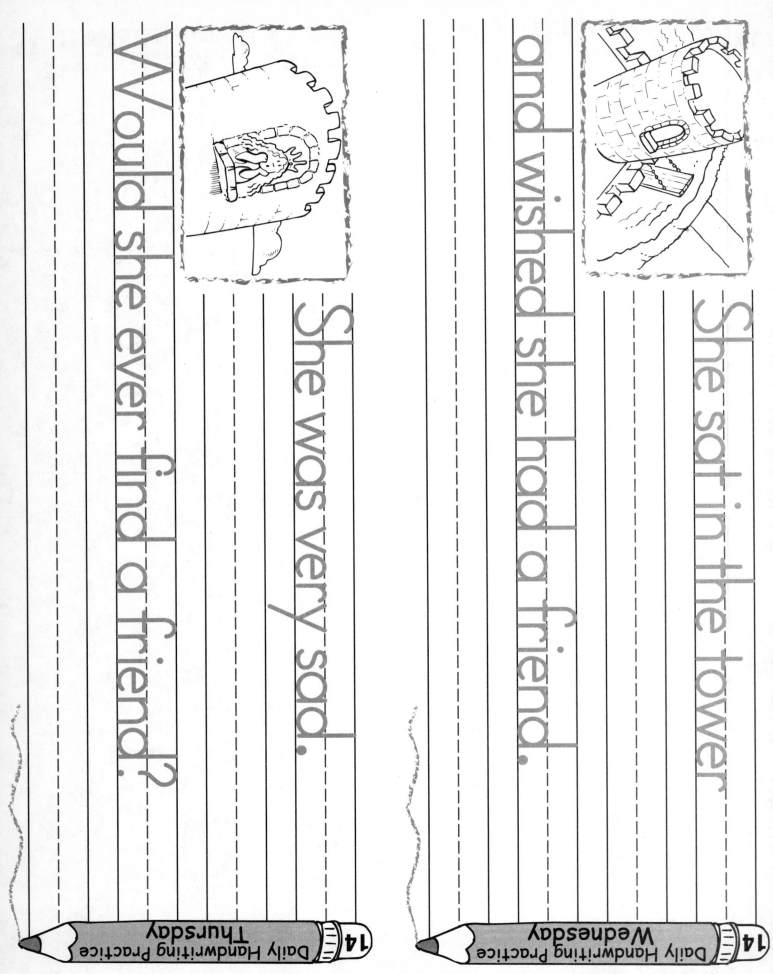

Would she ever find a friend?

She was very sad.

She sat in the tower

and wished she had a friend.

EMC 6844 • © Evan-Moor Corp.

The Princess

Once upon a time there was a beautiful princess. She lived in a castle with a moat. She had no visitors. She was lonely.

Finish the story.

Word Box

handsome prince

snuggly kitten

happily ever after

Tuesday

2

Tuesday
Tuesday
Tuesday

Today is terrific Tuesday.

Monday

1

Monday
Monday
Monday

Today is marvelous Monday.

Wednesday

Wednesday

Today is wacky Wednesday.

Wednesday 3

Thursday

Thursday

Today is thrilling Thursday.

Thursday 4

What a Week!

Today is Friday.
Finally, a fun-filled Friday.
We had a marvelous Monday,
a terrific Tuesday,
a wacky Wednesday,
and a thrilling Thursday.

Today is Friday.

What kind of pizza do you like?

veggie

cheese

peperoni

I like

What kind of sandwich do you like?

ham

tuna

peanut butter

I like

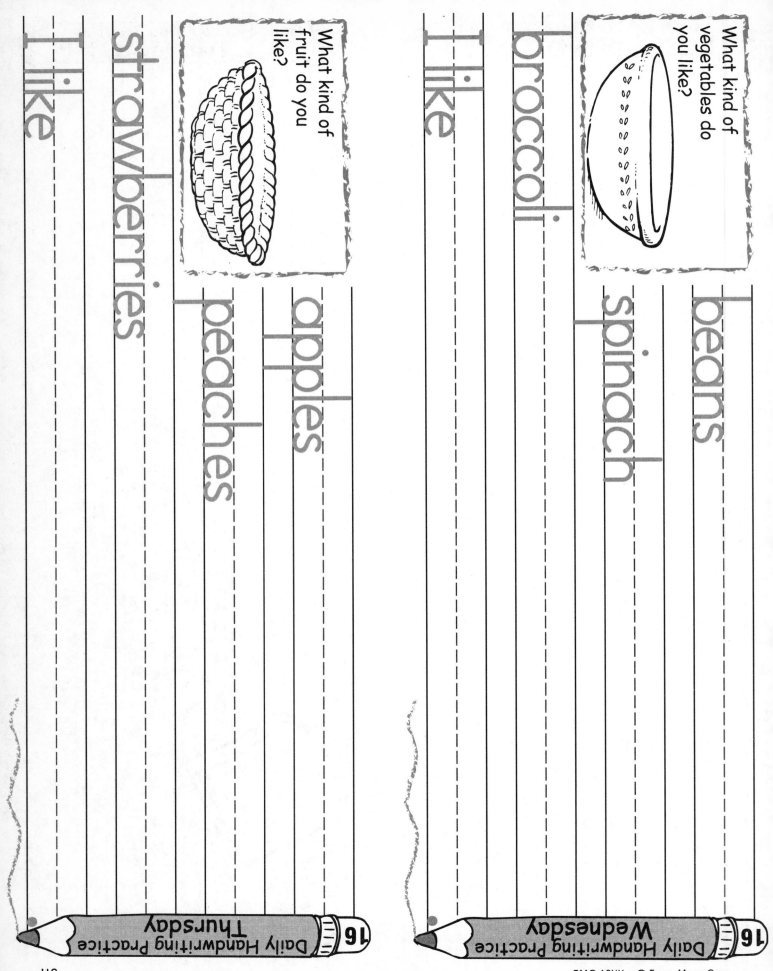

What kind of vegetables do you like?

beans

spinach

broccoli

I like

I like

What kind of fruit do you like?

strawberries

apples

peaches

I like

I like

Cooking

Copy this poem.

Measure and pour.
Stir it to mix.
Look at the things
That I can fix.

Pudding, pretzels
Sandwiches, too.
I think it's fun
To cook for you.

There were five in the nest
When there came a request.
Move over! Move over!
So the five moved over
And one fell out.

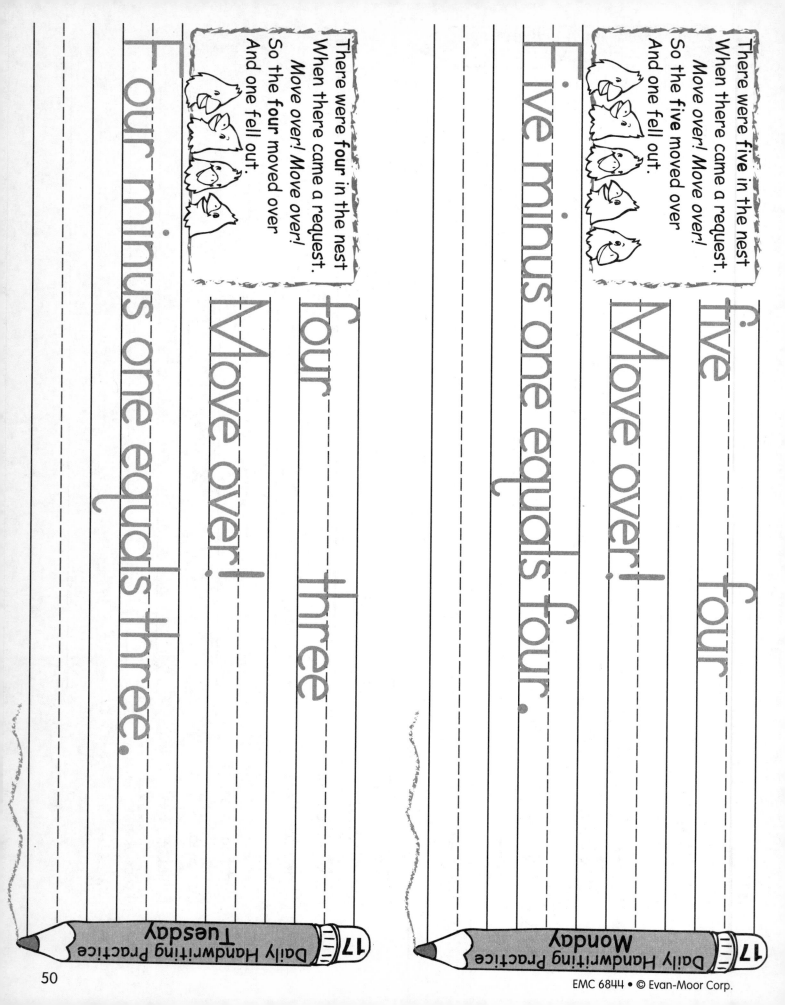

five

four

Move over!

Five minus one equals four.

There were four in the nest
When there came a request.
Move over! Move over!
So the four moved over
And one fell out.

four

three

Move over!

Four minus one equals three.

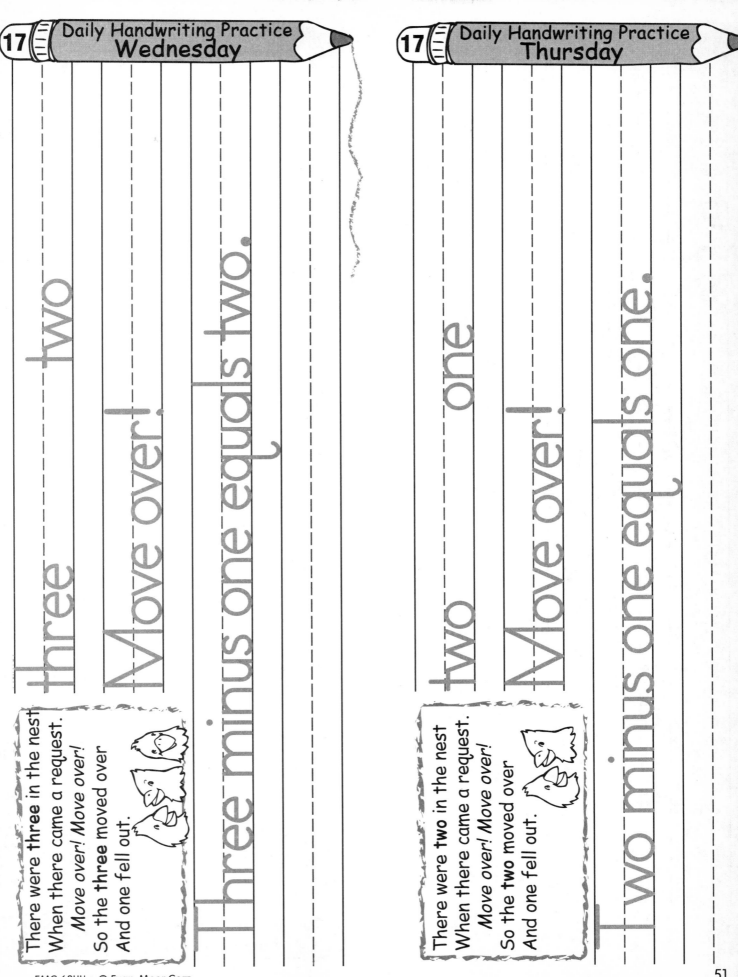

Wednesday

three

two

Move over!

Three minus one equals two.

There were **three** in the nest
When there came a request.
Move over! Move over!
So the **three** moved over
And one fell out.

Thursday

two

one

Move over!

Two minus one equals one.

There were **two** in the nest
When there came a request.
Move over! Move over!
So the **two** moved over
And one fell out.

Trace and write the numbers.

five

four

three

two

one

Sweet dreams.

Sleep tight.

There was one in the nest
And, at last, no request.
Just a quiet time for rest.
Shhhhh.

52

18 Daily Handwriting Practice
Monday

curves

corners

Shapes have curves or corners.

18 Daily Handwriting Practice
Tuesday

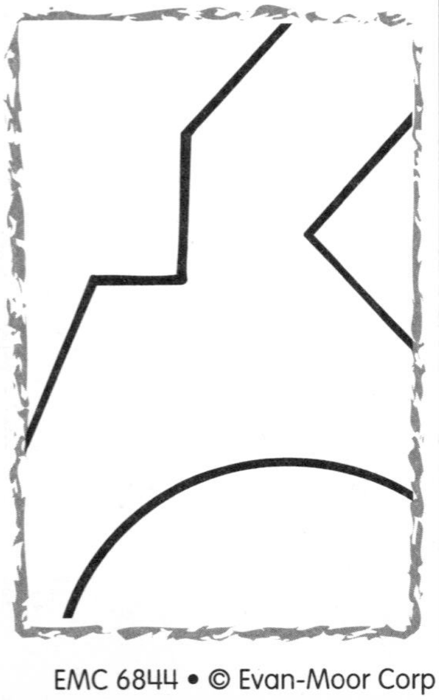

circle

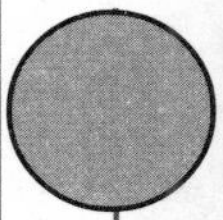

square

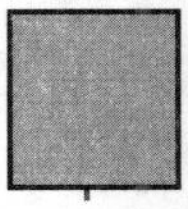

triangle

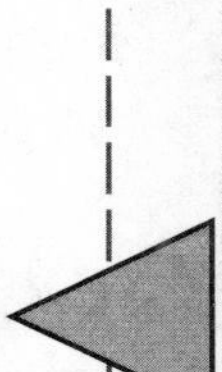

Name the shapes.

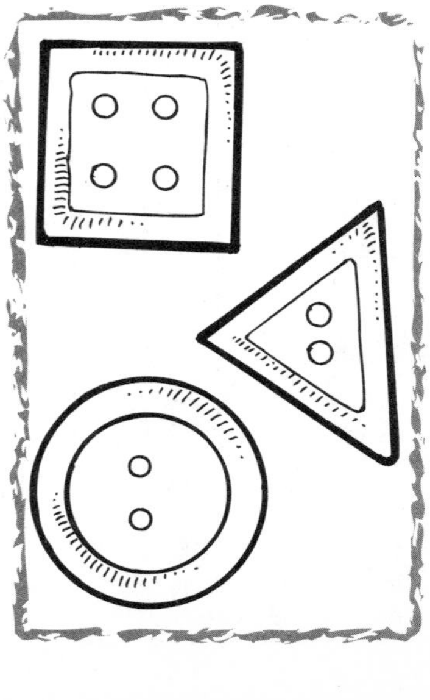

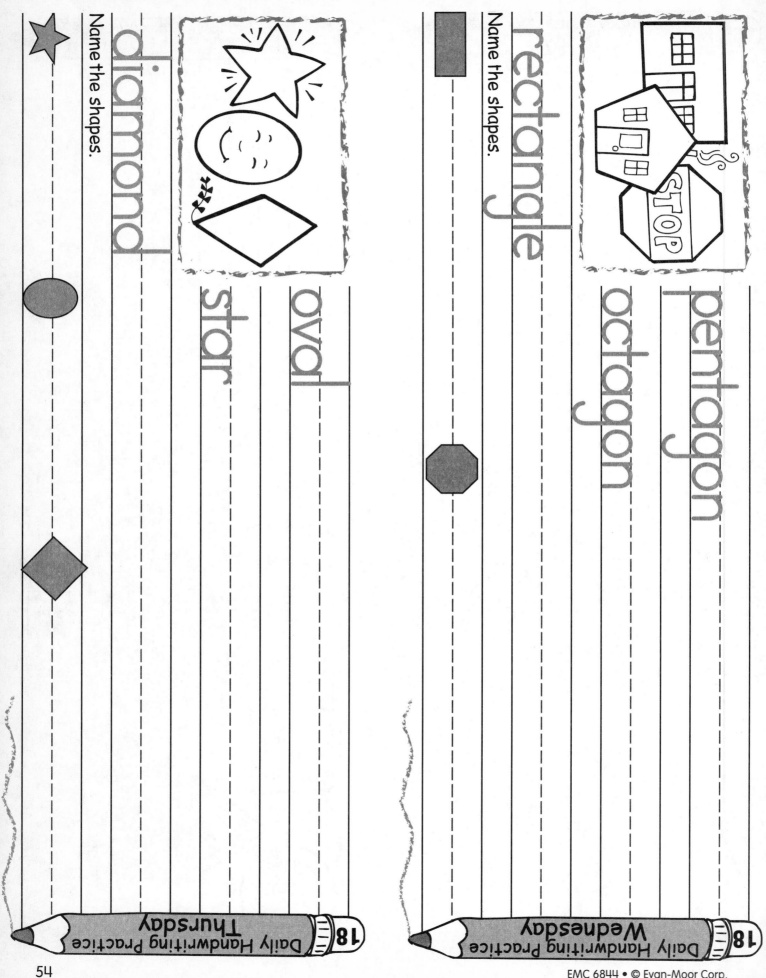

Name the shapes.

rectangle

pentagon

octagon

Daily Handwriting Practice
Wednesday

Name the shapes.

diamond

oval

star

Daily Handwriting Practice
Thursday

54

EMC 6844 • © Evan-Moor Corp.

Trace and finish the picture.

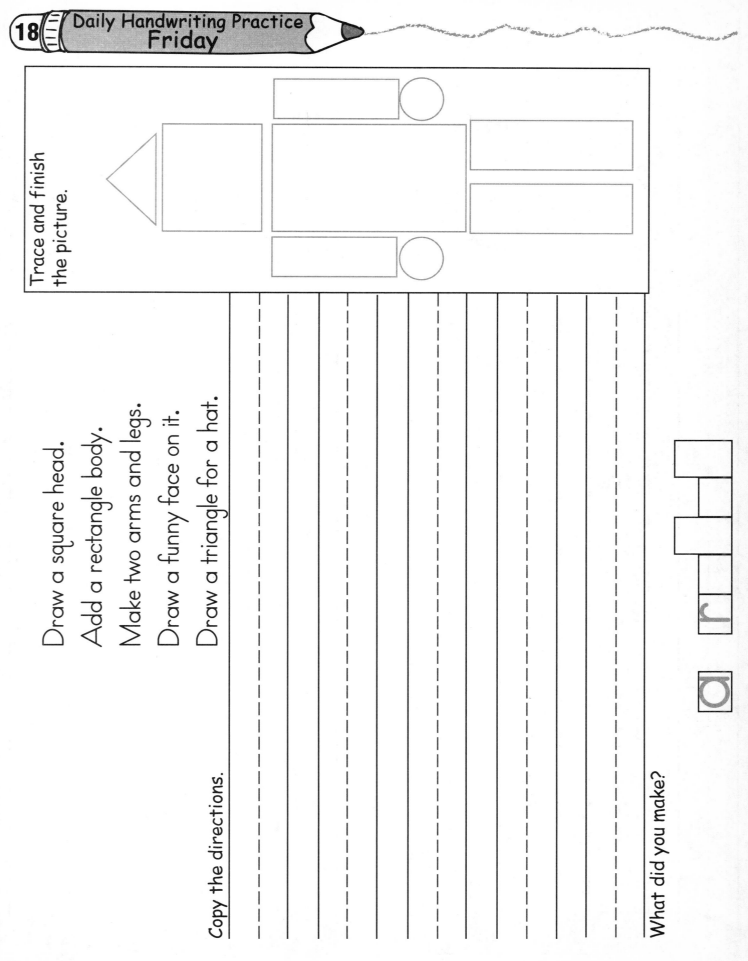

Draw a square head.
Add a rectangle body.
Make two arms and legs.
Draw a funny face on it.
Draw a triangle for a hat.

Copy the directions.

What did you make?

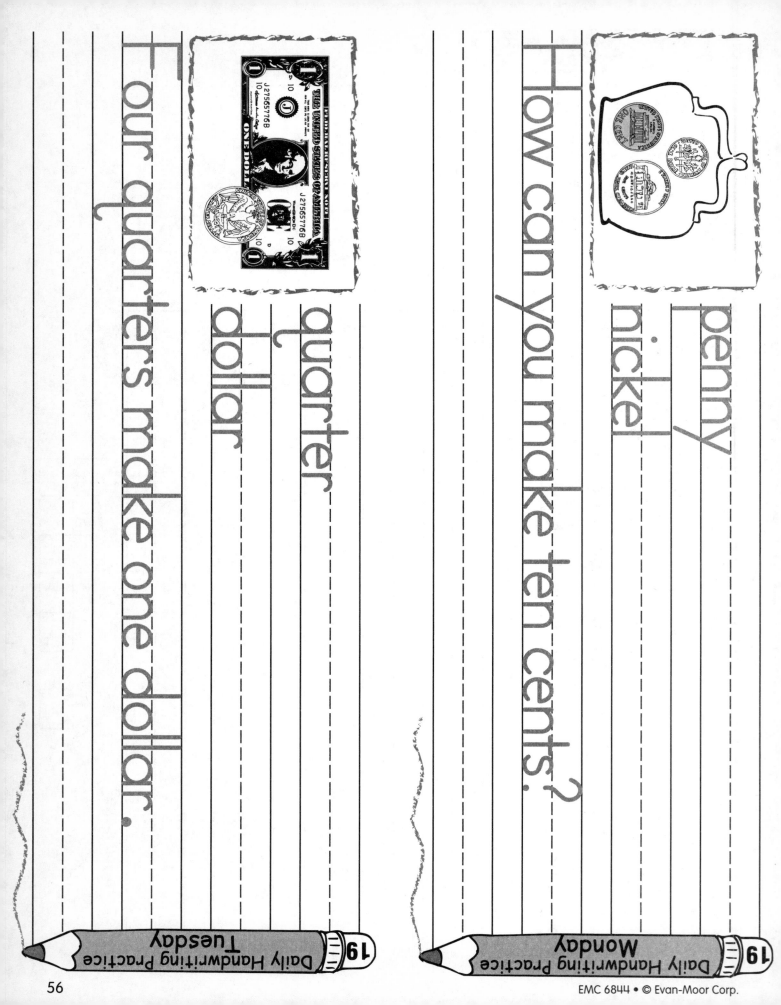

penny

nickel

How can you make ten cents?

quarter

dollar

Four quarters make one dollar.

dollar

bills

I carry my dollar bills in a wallet.

coins

change

Put your coins in the bank.

Mom keeps her money in a purse.
Dad keeps his money in his pocket.
Granny keeps her money in a pouch.
Buster keeps his money in a bank.

Money

Where do you keep your money?

first

second

I do won first place at the fair.

third

fourth

The gray ant is in third place.

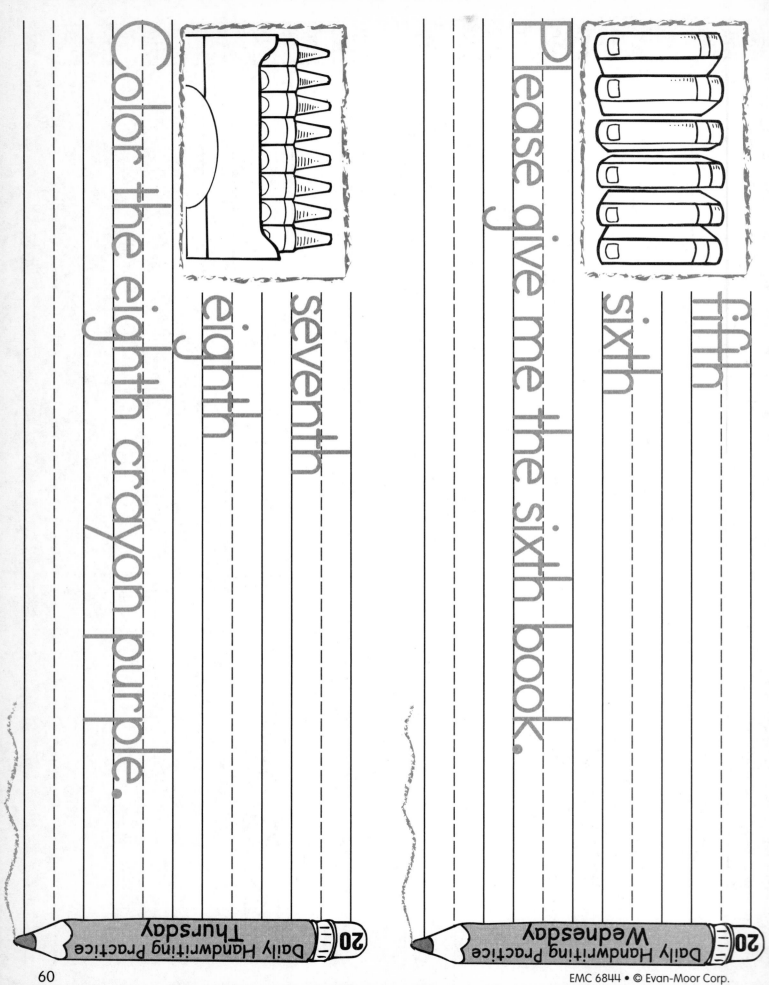

fifth

sixth

Please give me the sixth book.

seventh

eighth

Color the eighth crayon purple.

EMC 6844 • © Evan-Moor Corp.

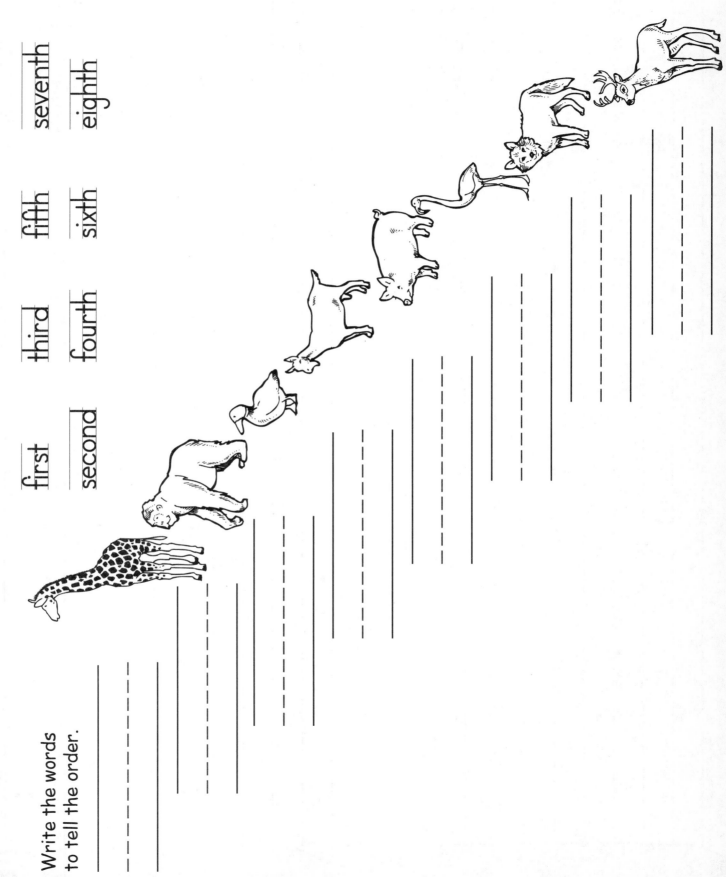

first   third   fifth   seventh
second fourth sixth   eighth

Write the words
to tell the order.

The birds flew over and under.

over

under

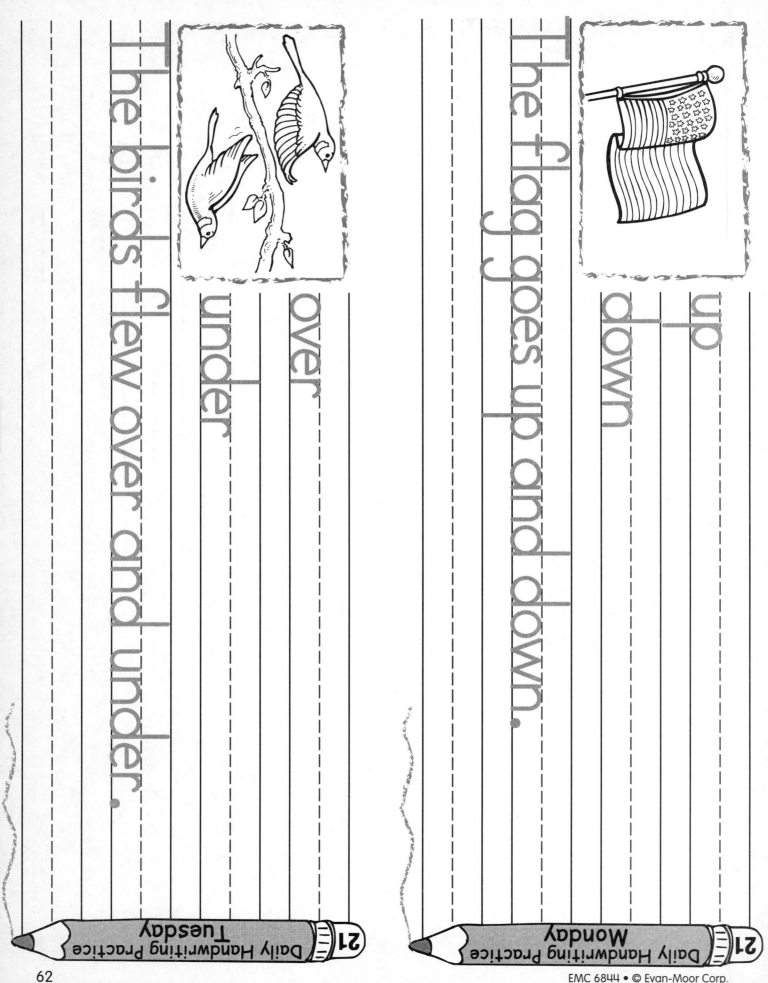

The flag goes up and down.

up

down

behind

in front

The goat is behind the gate.

above

below

One is above. One is below.

Singing in the Rain

Match the opposites.

up   behind

in front of   under

over   below

above   down

Copy the sentences to tell about the picture.

The bird is above the mushroom.

_____

_____

The mouse is below the mushroom.

_____

_____

The fence is behind the mushroom.

_____

_____

The leaf is in front of the mushroom.

_____

_____

alphabetical order

Dawn, Bert, Deb, Amy, Evan

Write the names in *ABC* order.

I know ABC order.

Joe, Hank, Kent, Lian, Fran

Write the names in *ABC* order.

Write the names in ABC order.

Rosa, Peg, Olaf, Said, Quan

I use ABC order.

Write the names in ABC order.

Zach, Tala, Will, Vicki, Uri

At the end is x, y, z.

Write the letters of the alphabet.

Aa

Cc

Nn

Ww

mothers

fathers

Moms and dads are parents.

We love our grandparents.

grandparents

Grandma   Grandpa

uncles

aunts

Uncles and aunts visit us.

relatives

reunion

You see relatives at a reunion.

The Family Reunion

Happy smiles,
Lots of names,
Yummy food,
Crazy games,
Hugs and kisses,
Teary eyes,
Handshakes, backslaps,
Warm good-byes.

Copy the poem.

our solar system

eight planets and one sun

Mars

Mercury

Venus

These planets are smaller than Earth.

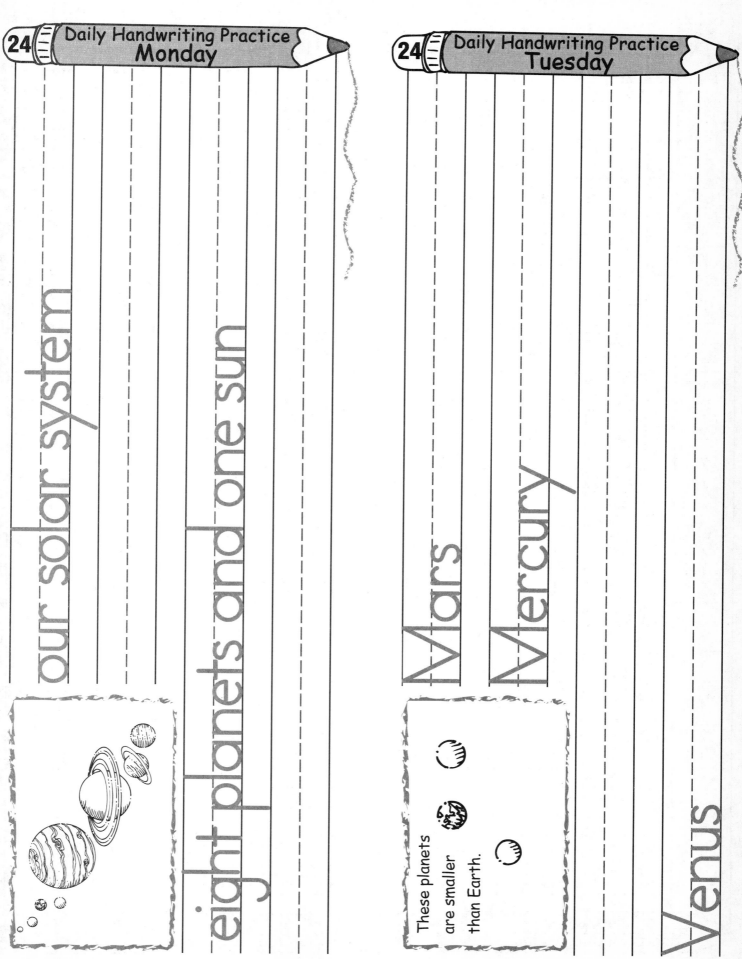

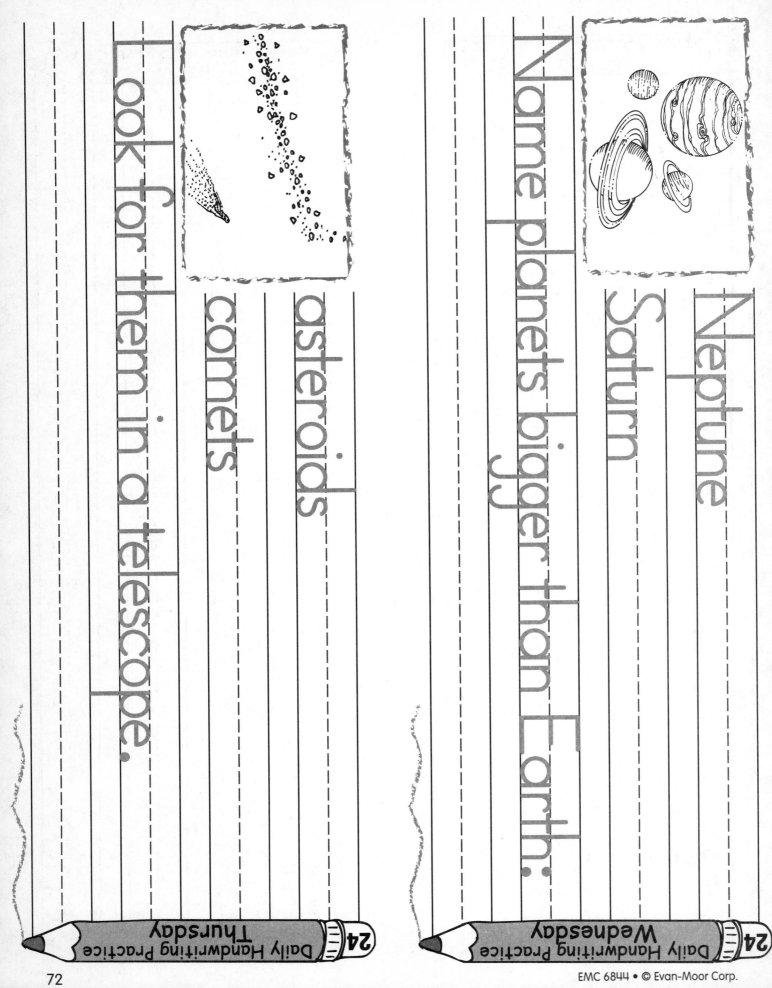

Name planets bigger than Earth.

Neptune

Saturn

Look for them in a telescope.

asteroids

comets

Our Solar System

Write the names of the planets.

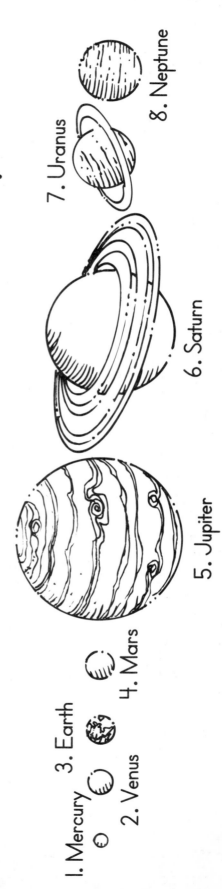

1. Mercury   3. Earth
2. Venus   4. Mars

5. Jupiter

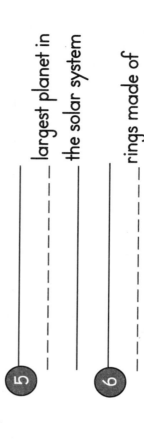

6. Saturn

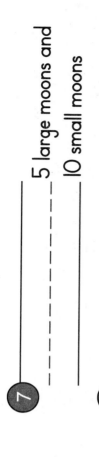

7. Uranus

8. Neptune

5 — largest planet in the solar system

6 — rings made of ice and rock

7 — 5 large moons and 10 small moons

8 — ball of gas with a center of rock and iron

1 — a small, rocky planet

2 — covered in thick, yellow clouds

3 — third planet from the sun

4 — soil is full of rust-colored iron dust

There are
12 months
every year.
See how well I write
them here.

The first three
months are:

January

February

March

There are
12 months
every year.
See how well I write
them here.

The next three
months are:

April

May

June

Daily Handwriting Practice
Wednesday
25

There are
12 months
every year.
See how well I write
them here.

July

August

September

The next three
months are:

Daily Handwriting Practice
Thursday
25

There are
12 months
every year.
See how well I write
them here.

October

November

December

The last three
months are:

The Calendar

Write the names of the months in order.

May	January	August
December	July	November
June	October	February
April	September	March

Save the Earth.

It is our job to use resources wisely.

Help reduce waste.

Help reduce trash and garbage.

Remake the old into new things.

Recycle your trash.

Reuse things at home.

Turn your trash into treasures.

Save the Earth

Make a plan for helping to protect our environment. Write what you will do. Use your best handwriting.

I will reduce.

I will reuse.

I will recycle.

I will

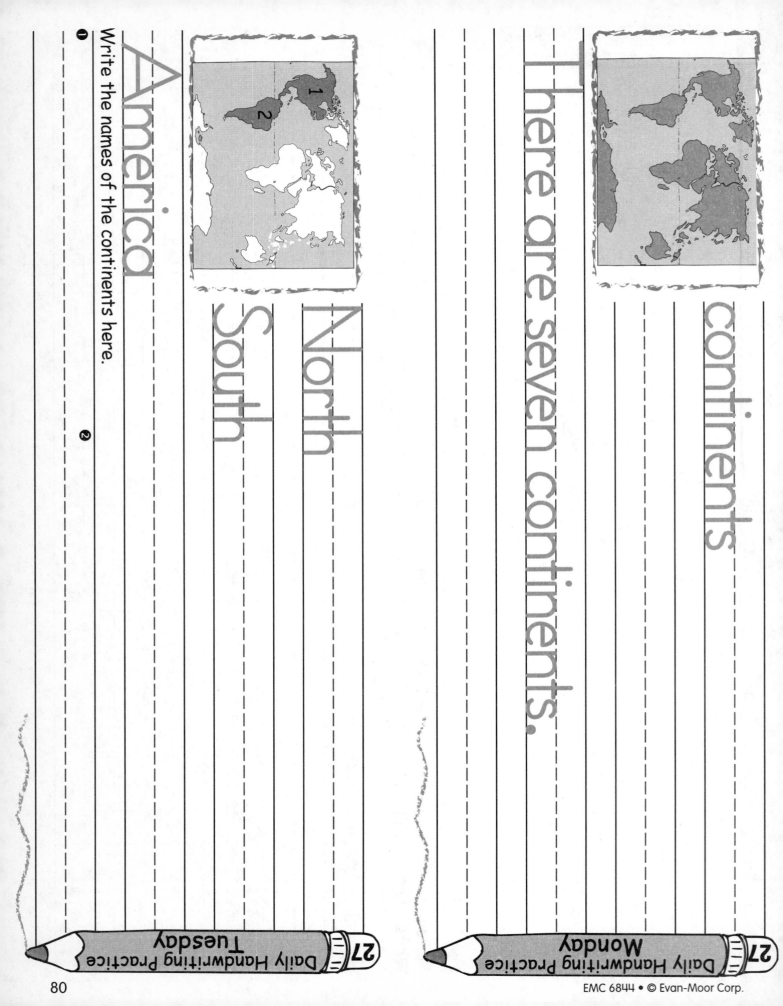

Monday

continents

There are seven continents.

Tuesday

North

South

America

Write the names of the continents here.

1

2

Australia

Antarctica

Write the names of the continents here.

❸

❹

Asia

Europe

Africa

Write the names of the continents here.

❺

❻

❼

Label the continents.

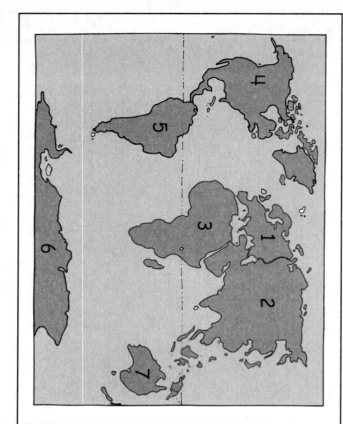

Africa   Antarctica
North America   Asia
South America   Australia
Europe

1
2
3
4
5
6
7

On which continent do you live?

I live on

rock

soil

Rock and soil form the crust.

The outside layer of the Earth is called the crust.

crust

mantle

metal

The mantle is below the crust.

The mantle is made of rock and metal.

mantle

The core is under the mantle.

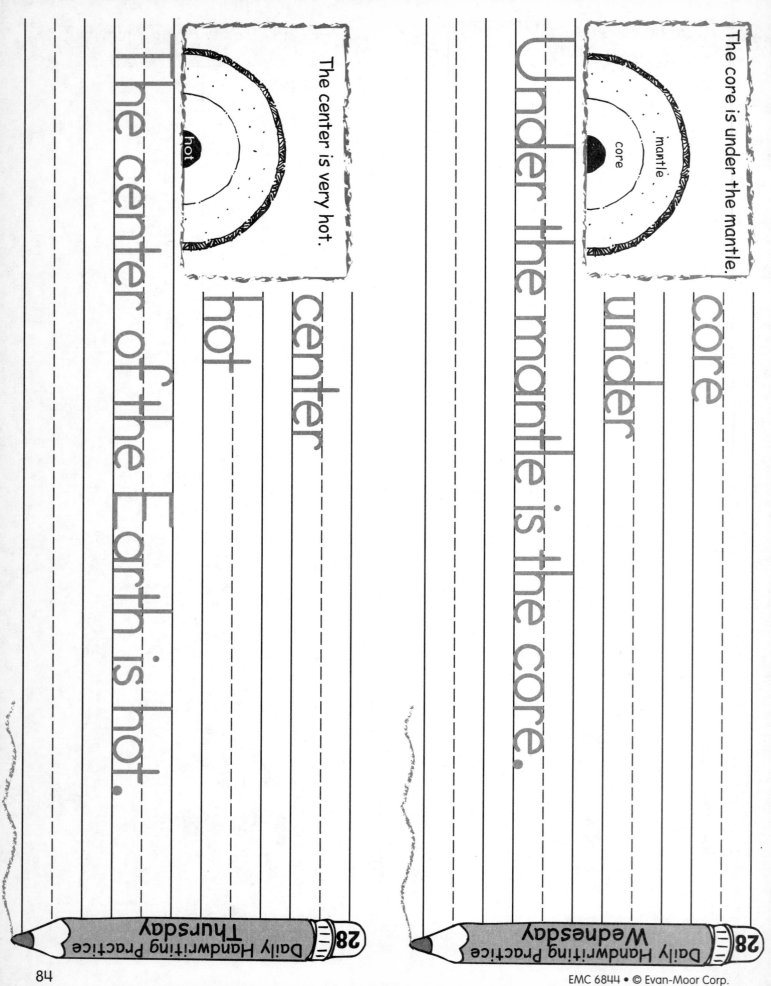

core

under

Under the mantle is the core.

The center is very hot.

hot

center

The center of the Earth is hot.

Earth's Layers

Label the Earth's layers.

1

2

3

4

We walk on the Earth's

crust   core   mantle   center

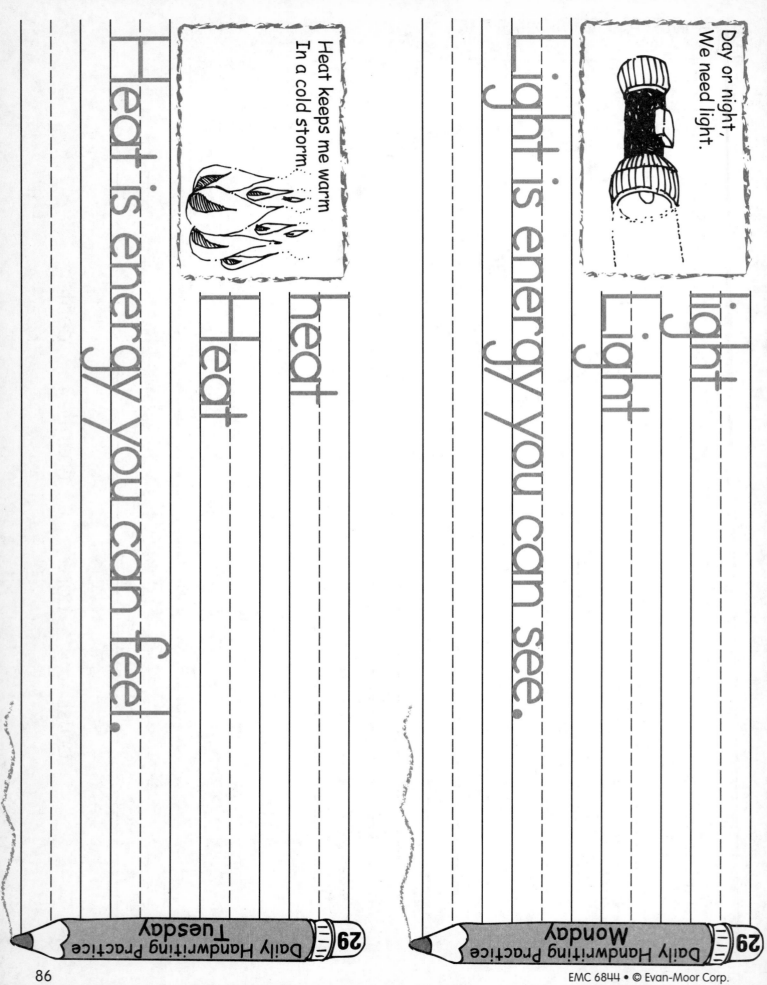

Day or night,
We need light.

light
Light

Light is energy you can see.

Heat keeps me warm
In a cold storm.

heat
Heat

Heat is energy you can feel.

sound

Sound

Sound is energy you can hear.

Just use your ear.
It's loud and clear.

energy

Energy

Energy has different forms.

Light, heat,
and sound
are all forms
of energy.

Energy Is All Around Us

Energy is all around us.
The light you see is energy.
The sound you hear is energy.
The heat you feel is energy.
Energy is all around us.

Copy the information.

fraction

fractions

A fraction is part of a whole.

Fractions have to be equal pieces.

one-half

two halves

The cupcake is divided into halves.

When something is divided into two equal pieces, the pieces are called halves.

When something is divided into three equal pieces, we call the pieces **thirds.**

third

thirds

The pie is divided into thirds.

When something is divided into four equal pieces, we call the pieces **fourths.**

fourth

fourths

The pizza is divided into fourths.

Fractions

three-fourths

two-thirds

one-third

Write how much is shaded.

one-fourth

one-half

soccer

golf

Hit the golf ball with a club.

baseball

football

Hit the baseball with the bat.

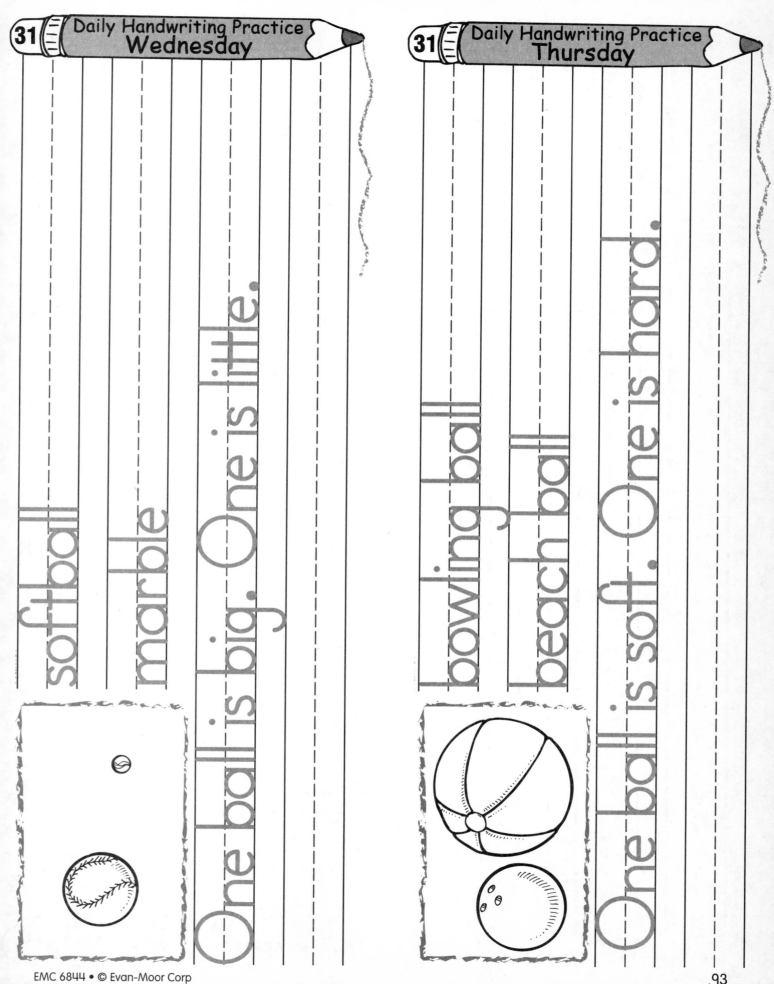

softball

marble

One ball is big. One is little.

bowling ball

beach ball

One ball is soft. One is hard.

Let's Play Ball!

Hit them. Catch them.
Throw them back.
Hike them to the
Quarterback.

Kick them. Roll them.
Blow them up.
Put them into the
Little cup.

Copy the poem.

roll

flatten

I can flatten my clay.

Roll out the clay.
It's time to play.

coil

fold

I can shape my clay into a pot.

Make a long snake
Or a pat-a-cake.

Bake your project
in the sun
Or in an oven when
you're done.

bake

fire

I can bake my clay in the sun.

Brush on the shine.
It looks mighty fine.

paint

glaze

I can brush paint on my clay.

96

What You Need

- bowl
- spoon
- 4 scoops of flour
- 1 scoop of salt
- 1 ½ scoops of warm water

What You Do

1. Dissolve the salt in warm water.
2. Stir as you add the flour.
3. Knead the dough for 5 minutes.
4. Put the dough into a plastic bag.

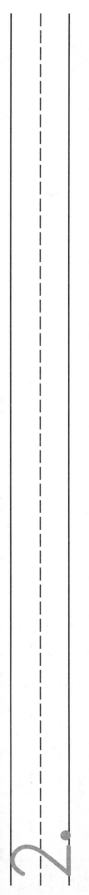

Baker's Clay

Copy the steps here that tell what to do.

1.

2.

3.

4.

33

Monday

Aa
army
ambulance

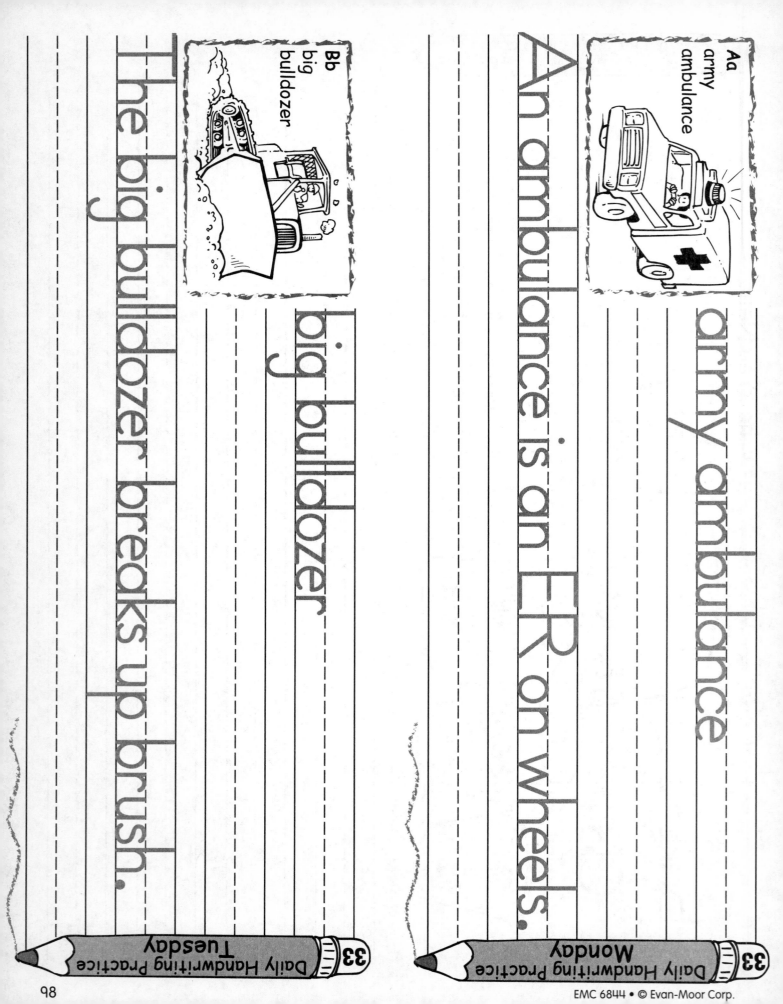

army ambulance

An ambulance is an ER on wheels.

EMC 6844 • © Evan-Moor Corp.

Tuesday

Bb
big
bulldozer

big bulldozer

The big bulldozer breaks up brush.

98

cozy carriage

The carriage coasts down the hill.

Cc
cozy
carriage

Caution:
Be careful with
your carriage.

dusty dump truck

The dump truck delivers dirt.

Dd
dusty
dump truck

Ee
early
elevated
train

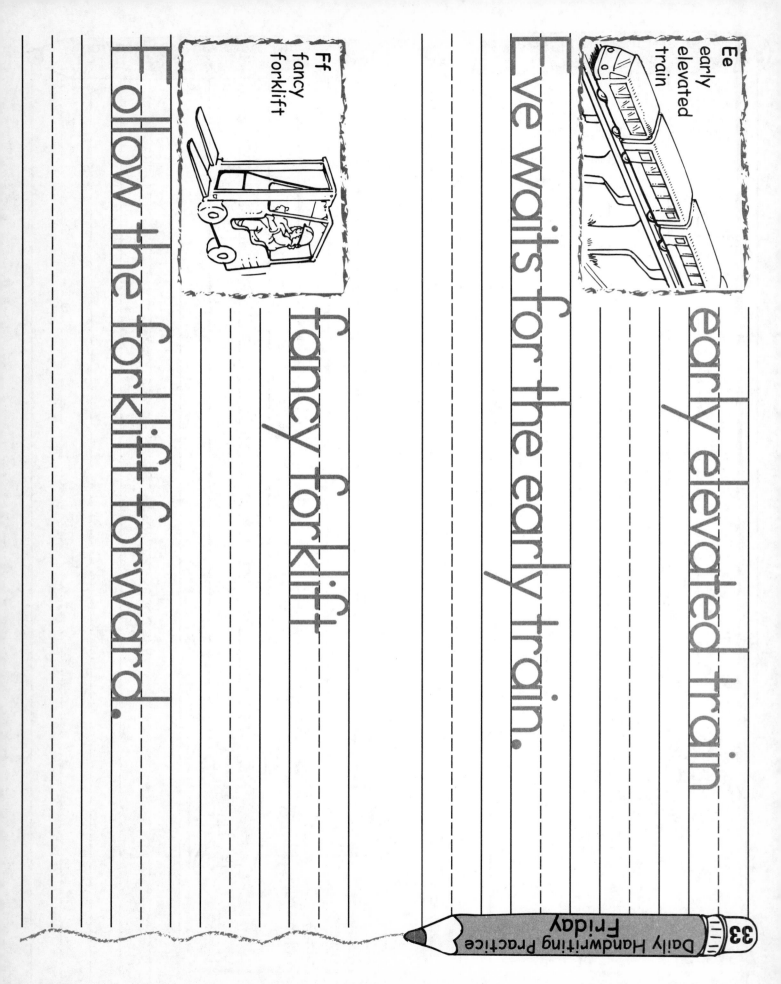

early elevated train

I've waits for the early train.

Ff
fancy
forklift

fancy forklift

Follow the forklift forward.

100

gas-gulping go-cart

Go get some gas for the go-cart.

Gg
gas-gulping
go-cart

high-flying helicopter

The helicopter hovers nearby.

Hh
high-flying
helicopter

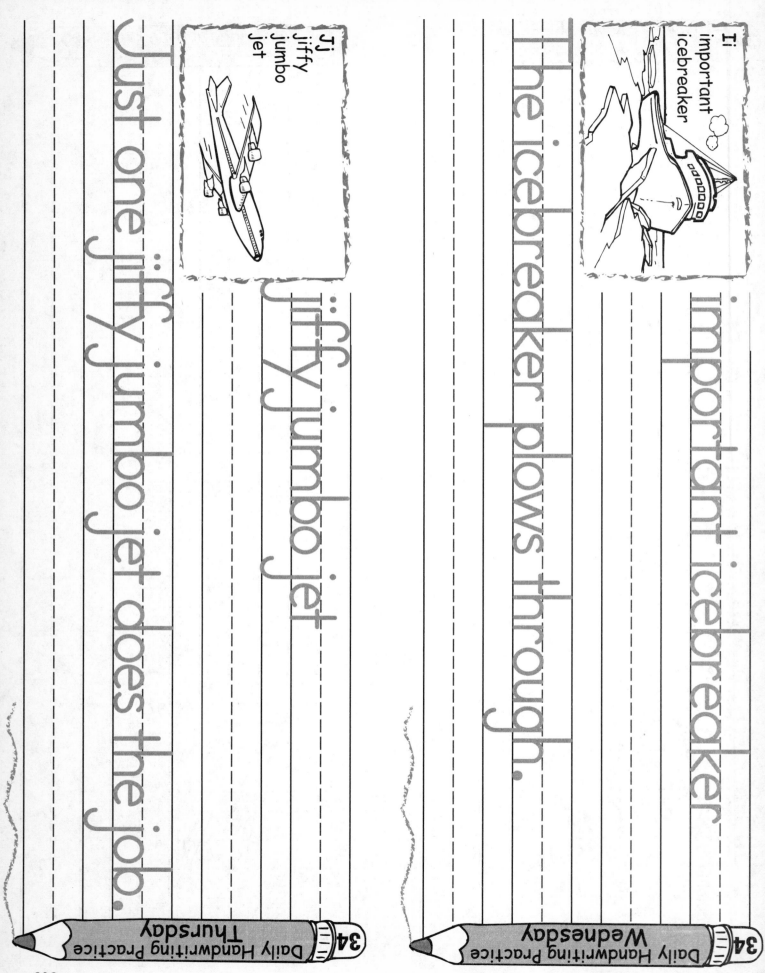

Ii
important
icebreaker

important icebreaker

The icebreaker plows through.

Jj
jiffy
jumbo
jet

jiffy jumbo jet

Just one jiffy jumbo jet does the job.

keen kayak

A kayak is a kind of canoe.

Kk
keen
kayak

long limousine

The long limousine led the line.

Ll
long
limousine

new
nuclear sub

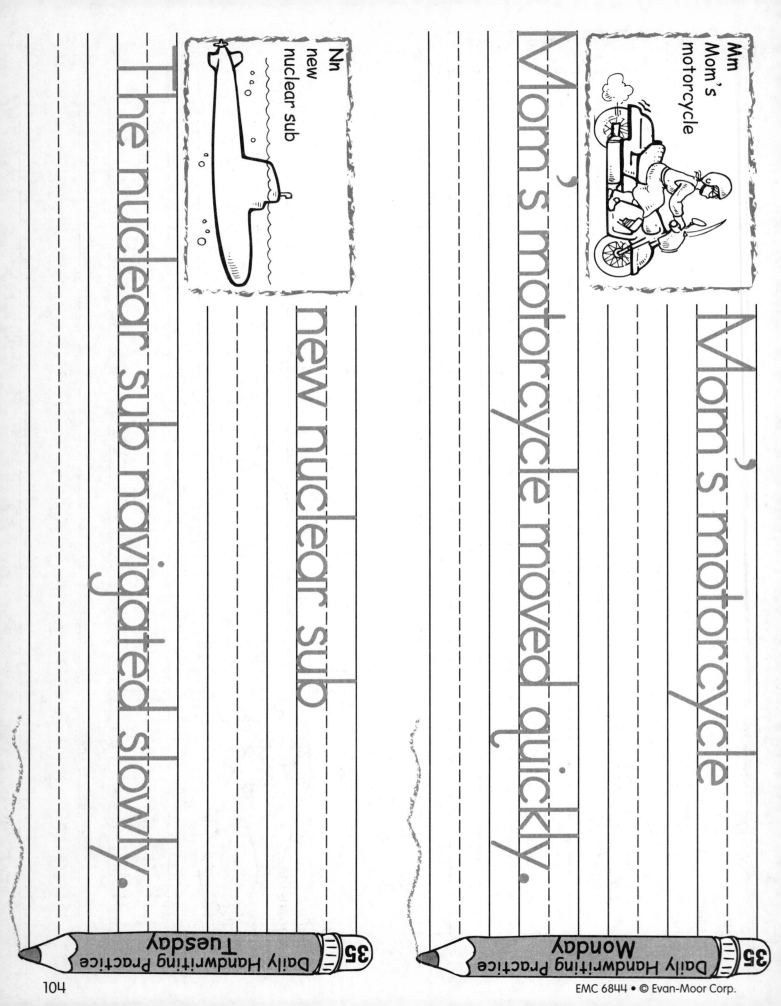

new nuclear sub

The nuclear sub navigated slowly.

Mom's
motorcycle

Mom's motorcycle

Mom's motorcycle moved quickly.

orange oil tanker

The oil tanker sailed out to sea.

Oo
orange
oil tanker

purple pickup

The pup rode in the purple pickup.

Pp
purple
pickup

Qq
quiet
QE II

quiet QE II

The QE II is an ocean liner.

Rr
racing
roadster

racing roadster

The roadster roared up the road.

106

EMC 6844 • © Evan-Moor Corp.

strong steamroller

The steamroller squashed the dirt.

Ss
strong
steamroller

tall trolley

The trolley travels on the tracks.

Tt
tall
trolley

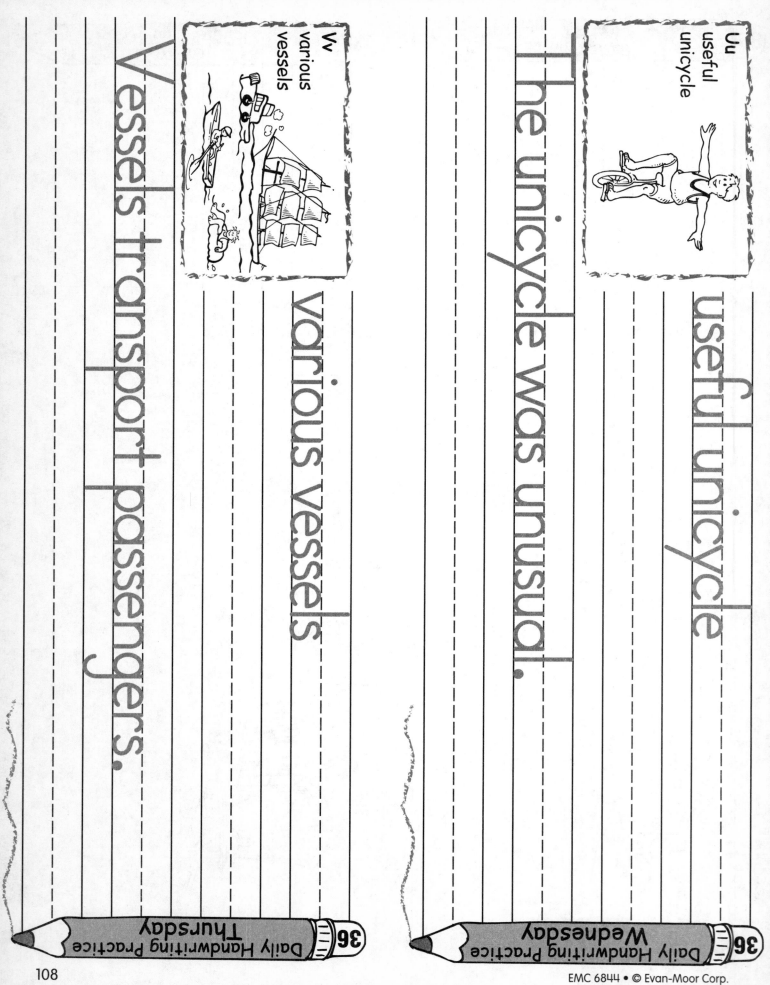

Thursday

Vv various vessels

various vessels

Vessels transport passengers.

Wednesday

Uu useful unicycle

useful unicycle

The unicycle was unusual.

Ww
white
wheelbarrow

white wheelbarrow

The wheelbarrow helped me work.

Xx
exciting
XK120

exciting XK120

The XK120 is a sports car.

Yy
yellow
yacht

yellow yacht

Yvette yearns for the yellow yacht.

Zz
zooming
Zero

zooming Zero

The Zero was a real plane.

Daily Handwriting Practice

Daily Handwriting Practice